MW01043480

WORLD OF **WoW** WONDER

THE AWESOME BOOK OF

TORNADOES AND OTHER STORMS

Get ready to hear your kids say, "Wow! That's awesome!" as they dive into this fun, informative, question-answering series of books! Students—and teachers and parents—will learn things about the world around them that they never knew before!

This approach to education seeks to promote an interest in learning by answering questions kids have always wondered about. When books answer questions that kids already want to know the answers to, kids love to read those books, fostering a love for reading and learning, the true keys to lifelong education.

Colorful graphics are labeled and explained to connect with visual learners, while entertaining explanations of each subject will connect with those who prefer reading or listening as their learning style.

This educational series makes learning fun through many levels of interaction. The in-depth information combined with fantastic illustrations promote learning and retention, while question and answer boxes reinforce the subject matter to promote higher order thinking.

Teachers and parents love this series because it engages young people, sparking an interest and desire in learning. It doesn't feel like work to learn about a new subject with books this interactive and interesting.

This set of books will be an addition to your home or classroom library that everyone will enjoy. And, before you know it, you too will be saying, "Wow! That's awesome!"

"People cannot learn by having information pressed into their brains. Knowledge has to be sucked into the brain, not pushed in. First, one must create a state of mind that craves knowledge, interest, and wonder. You can teach only by creating an urge to know." - Victor Weisskopf

© 2014 Flowerpot Press

Contents under license from Aladdin Books Ltd.

Flowerpot Press
142 2nd Avenue North
Franklin, TN 37064

Flowerpot Press is a Division of Kamalu LLC, Franklin, TN, U.S.A. and Flowerpot Children's Press, Inc., Oakville, ON, Canada.

ISBN 978-1-4867-0261-9

Written by:
Kate Perry

Illustrators:
Peter Roberts
Jo Moore

American Edition Editor:
Johannah Gilman Paiva

Designer:
David West
Children's Books

American Redesign:
Jonas Fearon Bell

Copy Editor:
Kimberly Horg

Educational Consultant:
Jim Heacock

Printed in China.

All rights reserved.

CONTENTS

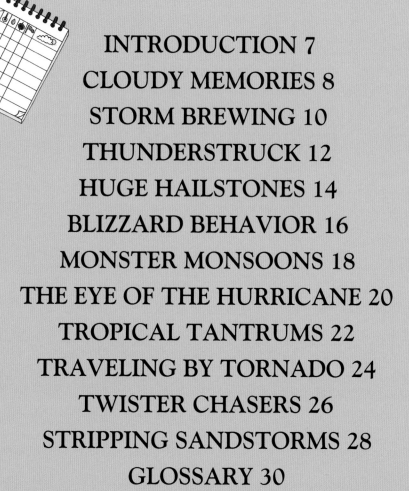

INTRODUCTION

Did you know that dust devils can be over half a mile (almost 1 km) high? That hurricanes can pile up boats like bath toys? That it can rain frogs, fish, and schoolchildren?

Discover for yourself amazing facts about severe weather, from the hailstone as big as a tennis ball (but much heavier!) to the storm surge that can fling boats over half a mile (over 1 km) inland.

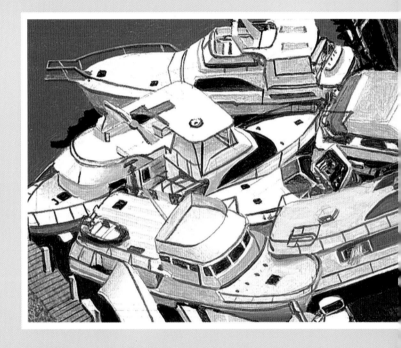

Look out for this symbol, which means there is a fun project for you to try.

True or false? Watch for this symbol and try to answer the question before reading on for the answer.

CLOUDY MEMORIES

The weather is a powerful force. William Rankin experienced this when he bailed out of his plane in a violent thunderstorm. He was bounced around in the clouds, battered by the wind for a terrifying 40 minutes before finally parachuting to safety.

In 1876, Denonath Sircar of Bangladesh clung to a broken branch all night to save himself in a flood that washed away millions of homes.

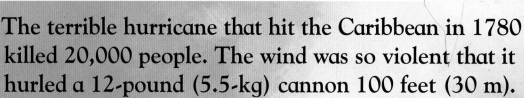

The terrible hurricane that hit the Caribbean in 1780 killed 20,000 people. The wind was so violent that it hurled a 12-pound (5.5-kg) cannon 100 feet (30 m).

Deanna Wyant and her
boyfriend actually flew around
the room when a tornado
hit their apartment in 1965.
The building collapsed, but
miraculously they both survived!

STORM BREWING

Thunderheads, or storm clouds, are called "cumulonimbus" clouds. "Cumulus" means "heaped" and "nimbus" means "rain cloud." You can see fluffy, low-level cumulus clouds building up into tall thunderclouds in warm weather. Some cumulonimbus clouds can be over nine miles (14.5 km) high.

Leave an upturned jar on a saucer of water in a sunny spot for an hour. The heat of the sun will cause some of the water to evaporate and rise as invisible water vapor. Watch the condensation forming on the glass as the invisible water vapor cools and it starts to "rain."

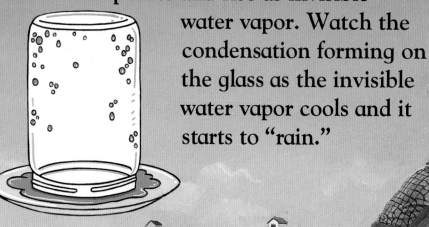

Cold, dry air

Warm, wet air

Clouds can be formed in many ways. In this case, a warm air mass moves in from the right. It rises over cold air moving in from the left. Rain forms where the masses meet.

3 The base of the cloud is low. The top is very high.

2 The air cools as it gets higher, and droplets form.

1 In hot weather, warm, wet air and dust rise to form cumulus clouds.

THUNDERSTRUCK

Thunder is the sound of lightning. The moving air inside a thundercloud builds up static electricity. This causes a huge flash of lightning that heats the air to 18,000°F (9,982°C). The air expands and explodes, making a thunderclap.

ONE AND
TWO AND
THREE AND

How far away is the storm? Count the seconds between the time when you see the lightning and the time when you hear the thunder. Count one mile for every five seconds (one kilometer for every three seconds).

Don't try Benjamin Franklin's famous 1752 experiment with a kite and a key to prove the electrical nature of lightning. A Swedish scientist, trying it out for himself in 1909, was electrocuted.

Reports of "ball lightning" have not been scientifically verified. A ball of lightning supposedly floated around a hotel room in France before drifting out of the window and exploding nearby.

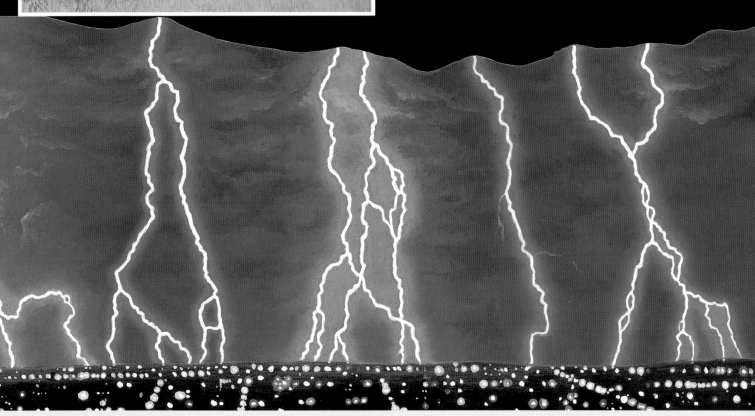

HUGE HAILSTONES

Some hailstones are the size of tennis balls. In India, these huge hailstones smashed car windshields, flattened crops, and killed thousands of birds. Many farmers now insure themselves against hail damage.

The largest hailstones fell during a storm in Bangladesh that killed 92 people in 1986. Each hailstone weighed up to two pounds (almost one kilogram).

True or false?
Firing shells at clouds can prevent hailstorms.

Answer: True
Anti-hail gunners in Uzbekistan fire shells at the sky, scattering tiny particles into the clouds. The smaller hailstones that cling to them melt before reaching the ground.

A hailstone has layers, like an onion. It picks up a layer of ice each time it goes up and down in the thundercloud.

Can you find the fish?

BLIZZARD BEHAVIOR

If you get stuck in a blizzard, lie down. This is a good survival tip, as the blanket of snow traps a layer of warm air around the body. Remember to make an airhole! Animals often survive in the snow this way.

Can you find the rucksack?

Snowflakes form when water vapor rapidly freezes as crystals around dust particles. Each snow crystal has six sides and each one is unique. Catch some on a dark glove and study them (quickly!) through a magnifying glass.

Avalanche! A weakness in a layer of snow on a slope or a precipice can start an avalanche. As thousands of tons of snow roar downhill, it can reach speeds of over 186 miles (300 km) per hour, burying everything in its path.

St. Bernard dogs were first kept by monks in the Swiss mountains to rescue people trapped in the snow. They wore barrels of brandy for reviving the patients.

MONSTER MONSOONS

A monsoon can last for up to six months. Water from the Indian Ocean evaporates in the winter and then falls as torrential rain in the summer monsoons. Farmers in low-lying parts of India can lose everything. In July, Bombay, India, gets eight times as much rain as New York City!

Showers of frogs have occurred in many places such as India and England! Other showers have included crabs, fish, and jellyfish.

Land is flooded when rain makes a river rise over its banks. Noah's flood is based on fact. There were floods in the Tigris-Euphrates valley in Turkey and Mesopotamia around 4000 B.C.

You can make your own rain gauge from a flat-bottomed plastic bottle. Find out how much rain falls in July where you live!

Top of plastic bottle is cut and placed upside down.

Measurements marked in inches (or cm).

Bottom filled with water to point where measure starts.

THE EYE OF THE HURRICANE

Hurricanes have eyes. The currents of air in a hurricane spiral upward to form a rotating circle of wind around a central "chimney." This calm center is called the "eye."

Can you find the satellite?

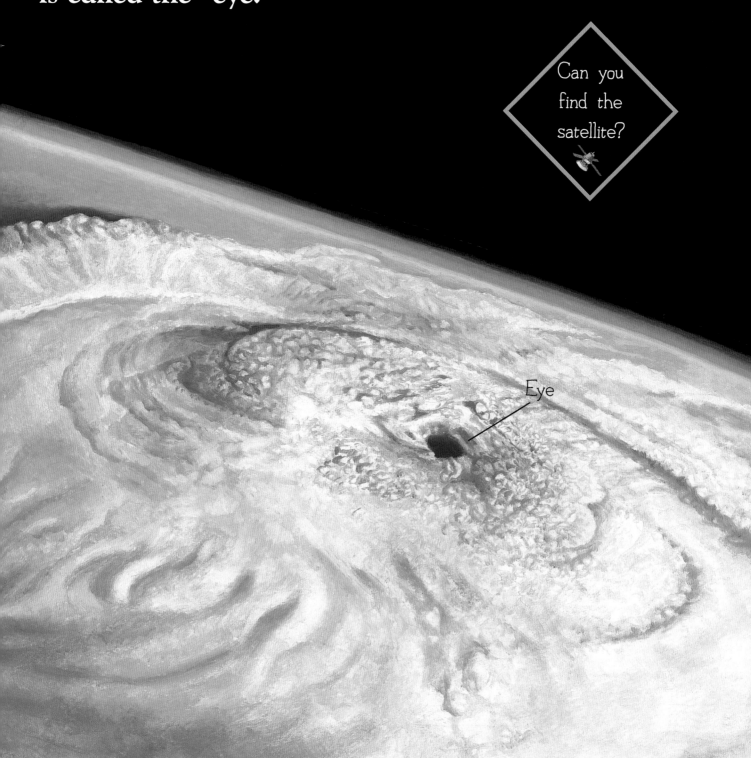

Eye

True or false?
Hurricanes are given girls' and boys' names.

Answer: True
Atlantic hurricanes are given alternate girls' and boys' names in alphabetical order from the beginning of the season. This makes them easier to reference.

Winds over 186 miles (300 km) per hour can cause unimaginable destruction. In 1992, Hurricane Andrew hit an area south of Florida, tearing roofs and walls off houses, smashing trees and cars, and piling up boats like little plastic toys!

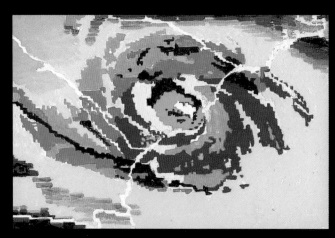

Infrared pictures from satellites provide color-coded information about tropical storms. Scientists can usually track their progress and warn people in time to prepare.

TROPICAL TANTRUMS

Typhoons can sink ships. Tropical storms can whip up mountainous waves. The highest wave ever measured was 85 feet (26 m), but the highest ever seen was 111 feet (34 m). Ships are helpless in such stormy seas.

Even a warship, such as an aircraft carrier, can crumple like tin in a typhoon. This is what happened to U.S.S. *Hornet* (right) near Okinawa, Japan, in 1945.

True or false? Hurricanes, tropical cyclones, and typhoons are all the same thing.

Answer: True
Tropical storms are called "hurricanes" in the Atlantic Ocean, "cyclones" in the Indian Ocean, "typhoons" in the China Sea, and "willy-willies" in Australia.

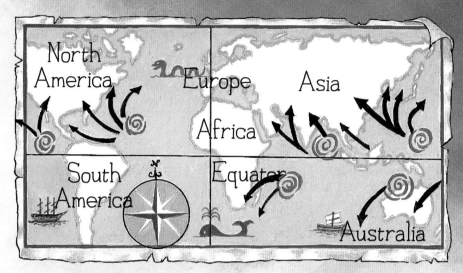

A storm surge carried this boat (below) nearly a half mile (three-quarters of a kilometer) inland. Huge waves can surge in ahead of a hurricane, flooding low-lying areas.

"Raining" fish are sucked up and carried far away before falling.

TRAVELING BY TORNADO

Tornadoes can make children fly. Tornadoes are small, ferocious storms. People, animals, and whole houses can be picked up and dropped some distance away. In 1986, 13 Chinese schoolchildren were carried 12 miles (19 km) by a tornado before being deposited completely unharmed!

Can you find 13 children?

A dust devil in the desert is a miniature tornado. Spinning winds whirl sand and dust to heights of between 300 and 3,000 feet (or 91 and 914 m).

A whirling cloud turns
into a waterspout as
water is sucked up.
It is spectacular, but not
terribly dangerous.

A tornado, or "twister,"
comes down out of
thunderclouds like an
"elephant's trunk"—
a spinning funnel of cloud
that sucks up dust and soil.
The funnel gets tighter and
the wind gets faster, up to
500 miles (805 km) per hour.

TWISTER CHASERS

People chase twisters. The more we understand about tornadoes, the easier it will be to predict when one is coming along. Scientists study tornadoes by following them and putting monitoring equipment in their path to assess their strength and learn as much about them as possible

True or false?
People can make their own twisters.

Answer: True
But not full-size ones! Japanese scientist Tetsuya Fujita studied miniature tornadoes made with dry ice. He developed the Fujita Scale, which rates tornado intensity.

An eyewitness described a tornado in 1928:
"The great shaggy end of the funnel hung directly overhead. There was a strong gassy odor. The walls were of rotating clouds with constant flashes of lightning that zigzagged from side to side." (see right)

This scientist fires a rocket into thunderclouds. Wires attached to the rocket trigger a charge of lightning.

STRIPPING SANDSTORMS

A sandstorm can easily strip the paint off a car. Loose dust and sand in deserts is whipped up by the wind, flinging millions of stinging grains at every surface. Sand-carrying winds carve desert rocks into strange shapes.

Sand-carved rock found in an American desert

Industrial sand-blasting is used to strip dirt and paint off old buildings to make them look new again.

A terrifying 9,000-foot-(2,743-m-) high storm turns the sky dark and sandblasts everything in its path.

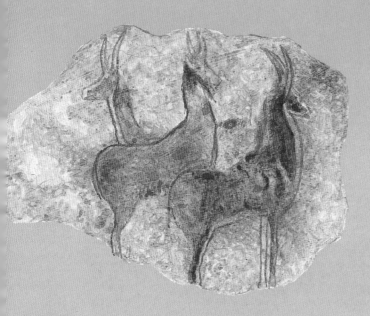

There were dust storms in the American Midwest in the 1930s. The rain failed and wind blew the dry soil around. Farmers couldn't grow anything, livestock died, and people left the region.

True or false?
The Sahara has always been a desert.

Answer: False
Climate can change. Cave paintings in the Sahara show that it was once home to all types of animals that could only live where there was water and grass.

GLOSSARY

Air pressure
The weight of the air pressing down on the land. High pressure usually means good weather and low pressure usually means bad weather.

Avalanche
Snow (or rocks or ice) falling rapidly down a mountainside.

Climate
The weather a particular place has come to expect over a long period of time.

Condensation
When a gas, such as water vapor, cools to form droplets of liquid. Clouds are formed this way with droplets of water.

Currents of air
Stream of air moving from a high to low pressure area.

Evaporation
When a liquid, such as water, is heated and turns into a gas that rises into the air.

Hailstones
Pieces of ice, formed in thunderclouds, that fall to the ground, often in warm weather.

Infra-red

Satellites can use infra-red rays to show the different heat patterns as pictures—clouds show up as bright (cold) and deserts as dark (hot).

Monsoon

The name of the south-westerly wind that brings heavy rain to parts of Asia in the summer; also the name given to the rainy season in those places.

Static electricity

Electricity that isn't flowing in a current. It builds up from friction (such as when you rub a balloon or stroke a cat), or from lots of activity in a cloud.

Storm surge

Waves blown before the wind that can cause flooding, especially if forced through a narrow channel.

Tropical storms

Violent storms that develop in the hot (over 80°F/27°C), moist air above warm seas near the Equator in summer and fall.

INDEX